The Story of My Life

by Dr. Charles S. Price

For more great Christian classics that have been out-of-print for far too long, visit us online at:

JawboneDigital.com

ISBN: 1548470678
ISBN-13: 978-1548470678

TABLE OF CONTENTS

1
MY BIRTH

Tall stand the smoke begrimed chimneys of old Sheffield. The great steel metropolis of the world is situated in the Midlands of England, a busy wide awake city set in a scene of entrancing beauty. Little Smithy Wood was in the suburbs. By the side of the lazy old mill pond stood the forge, with its anvils and furnaces, and back of it was the home where dwelt the family of Price. It was there that my father was born. It was there he spent his boyhood days.

Grandfather was a very large and muscular man, whose big arms were knotted because of his daily task of pounding the iron into shape while the sparks flew from the anvil.

The family was poor, but contented and happy. Four boys were born in that home, all of whom went into the steel business except one. That boy was the youngest, Charles. In later years he became my father. I am proud to have come from such a stock. My uncle Ben, the oldest of the boys, earned his daily bread by the sweat of his brow in one of the great steel mills not far from the place where he was born; but he was known throughout the length and breadth of the country-side as a great preacher, loved and honored and respected by all who knew him. There was hardly a Sunday but what he could be found occupying some pulpit. I was a small boy when the Lord took him home to glory, but never shall I forget his deep resonant "Hallelujah" that sounded through the church whenever he occupied the pulpit.

The second boy, Joe, like his brother, worked in the cutlery mills, and was also known throughout the country-side as a man very active in church work, and whose kind and loving disposition made him very much in demand among people who needed counsel and help.

Then came my Uncle Will. He held a very unique record. Over half a century ago as a young boy he went to apply for a position in one of the great English steel firms. He got the job and started to work at a certain bench. Fifty years went by and still he was working not only for the same firm, but at the same bench. When he visited this country in company with my father a few years ago he told me that every man employed by the steel firm when he first went into it was dead. Every one of the bosses was dead, but he was still working over the fires in the forge at the same place he started fifty years before.

He was very close to me. As a boy I always loved him dearly. What a joy it was to my heart that he was privileged to come to America with my father and see me laboring for the Lord Jesus on a continent so far away from the place I had called my home. He has gone home to glory now, leaving a splendid family who, like their father, are all servants of the Lord Jesus Christ. As a matter of fact, I do not know of a relative on either side of the family who has not been saved through the blood of Jesus.

My Father

My Father, Charles, was the youngest son. To see him today—to hear him speak—to look at the beautiful home in which he lives— you never would dream that his early years were ones of struggle and privation. He did not have at the beginning very many educational advantages. He left school when he was eleven, and went to work for the sum of fifty cents a week. He delivered groceries for a provision establishment, making his deliveries by pushing a little iron wheel truck noisily over cobble stone streets. He was genuinely saved when he was eleven years of age. He soon won the confidence of the master in the store and was promoted from an outside to an inside position. So convinced they were regarding his sincerity and honesty that at the early age of seventeen he was made the manager of a local branch. Then he fell in love with the girl who was to become my mother. She came from excellent stock. Her father was a building contractor in one of the suburban districts of the great steel city. They met at church and their interests were mutual. It was not long before they were married and started down life's pilgrim way together. Little did they dream of the sorrow that was to come in just a few short years.

My ambitious young father decided to enter business for himself. He had very little capital —practically nothing but a good name; which, after all, was of more value than money. A tiny little shop, not very much bigger than a good-sized living room, was rented and on an eventful Saturday the place was opened for business. When my father asked the representative of the wholesale house to what extent he could get credit the reply came without hesitation, "Your credit, Mr. Price, is unlimited. You can have all that you want and when you want it." Of such great value is a good name. It was on that opening Saturday that my Uncle Will, my father's older brother, marched into the grocery store and deposited a little bag upon the counter. In that bag were the savings of his lifetime. Looking my father in the eye, he said, "Charles, I brought this for you because I thought you might need it." Then he was gone. In those olden days family ties were strong and home life was something transcendently beautiful and sweet.

Birthplace

I was born on a quaint little English street in a little brick house that jostled right up to the sidewalk. There was no lawn in front and no gardens in the back. We did, however, have a back yard, which we had to share with our neighbors. With my birth, my hard-working father and loving mother both resolved that if God spared my life I should be given an opportunity that my father, at any rate, had never enjoyed. It was the opportunity of schooling and of education. It was not until later years that I discovered that my dear father worked for ten solid years without ever taking a holiday. At eight o'clock in the morning he would be behind the counter in the little shop and it would be eight o'clock at night before the shutters were closed and he would trudge wearily homeward. He would walk in order to save the money he would have to spend for the street cars. Every penny would count; for he had certain plans in store for me. On Saturday night it was eleven o'clock before the shop would close and then he would wend his way home to get a few hours sleep; for under no consideration could he miss Sunday school or church service in the morning. When I was two years of age my little sister Jessie was born. The arrival of the sweet baby was in a sense clouded with deep sorrow, for the birth of the child meant the death of my mother. I do not remember my mother; although there have been times, especially in later years, when she has seemed to be very, very near to me. Everyone who has ever spoken of her to me has commented on her beauty; but most of all upon the exquisite loveliness of her character. I have been told that before she went away to glory she took me in her arms and dedicated me to the service of the Lord. Sometimes we wait long before prayers are answered; but God did answer that prayer, many years later in a far distant city, six thousand miles away. One of these days, in the not too far distant future, I am going to have a real happy visit with the mother that I never knew.

Earliest Memories

There were days of hard struggle for my father after my mother died, but he toiled on and worked unceasingly with two children now to provide and plan for as they faced the future. My earliest memories are those of going to the home of my maternal grandmother. I can see her now as she was sitting in the little house on the hilly road that stands out vaguely through the mist of memory. I can also remember spending some of my time at the home of my grandmother on my father's side. I can see an open fireplace, a small smoke-begrimed oven, an old, old rocking chair and an old lady sitting in it with a quaint English cap of lace. I am reaching as far back as memory will take me into the distant past to bring up these pictures of long ago. The passing years frame memory's pictures with a sweetness that lingers in the heart.

2
MY BOYHOOD

A few years later another great event occurred in our little family. My father married again. It is my belief that he could have searched the world around and not found a sweeter or a nobler woman than the one I learned to call my mother. My first remembrance of her is when she knelt in prayer with my little sister Jessie and myself by her side. From the very beginning our home was a house of prayer. It began with prayer in the morning and when the sun set over the sleepy hills it was with prayer that my father closed the day. Never would we sit down to a meal but what the blessing of the Lord was asked upon the food and thanks were returned when the meal was over. Sunday was a day set apart especially for God and the church, and never a toy was allowed out in our home. Reading was permitted, but Sunday School must be attended twice every Sunday as well as the morning and evening worship in the church. It was in this kind of atmosphere that I grew up. My new mother was kindness, love and consideration itself. I became so attached to her that when one day a boy on the school grounds called her "stepmother" I indulged in my first fist fight, which I well remember, and came out victor, although a little the worse for wear.

My dear mother was very insistent that plans and preparation be made to give me the best schooling they could possibly afford. I first attended the Sharrow Lane Board School. I was all boy, very mischievous, rather inclined to be disobedient to my parents and, for some unaccountable reason, a born fighter; but I studied hard and applied myself to the task that was before me. The result was that I got ahead of my class and was promoted two grades at a time until I was enabled to enter high school at the age of twelve. Some studies were very hard for me, especially mathematics and science, but the dear Lord had blessed me with a remarkable memory. The principal of the school said that I could memorize verses faster and more accurately than anyone he had ever known. The things I memorized then, I can remember today. How I praise the Lord for this ability to retain things. What a help it has been to me in my ministry in these later years.

Just before I left grammar school an incident occurred that nearly robbed me of my chance to go to high school. Considerable rivalry existed between our school and another on a neighboring street. I organized the boys of our class. We put chunks of wood in our caps and then tying ropes around them I led forth my brave band of school boy warriors to battle, and to face the enemy. It was a battle all right. The next day we were sitting in the classroom looking rather the worse for the conflict, but jubilant because we had won the flight. The door opened and the principal stuck his head in the room. My heart commenced to pound. Then, as the smiling face of the principal beamed upon us, my heart took wings again. "Boys," he said, "we all love our grand old school. I understand there was a battle yesterday in the defense of the name of good old Sharrow Lane. Who was the brave Horatius, that led our boys to victory?" My face flushed. I did not know who Horatius was, but I figured he must be someone great and grand. The boy behind me tapped me with a ruler so I stood on my feet. "If you please, sir," I said, "I am the boy." The principal looked at me through his spectacles and said, "I thought as much, but I was not sure"; then I was carried to the office. What happened there need not be put in this record. Suffice it to say that my boast when I came out was that he could not make me cry. It was only after a good deal of pleading that my scholastic standing was restored. After that I studied harder and fought less.

High school days came and went. One of

my essays entitled "A Contrast" was sent to London. It attracted so much attention that it was translated into French and sent to the Paris Exposition. I became the editor of the school paper and on the advice of some of my tutors started to prepare myself for a career in law.

In spite of my disobedience and waywardness, I really loved my father and mother. Never shall I forget the night my father and I walked down one of the tree-lined avenues near our home and he poured out to me, from the fulness of his heart, the news that he was going to send me to college. It was not from his lips that I heard the complete story of the sacrifice he had made in order for me to go there. I got that later from my Uncle Will. The conversation I had with my father that night has lived with me through the years, and left an impression on me that has kept me more than once in times of storm.

College Days

When a few weeks later I walked up the stately stairs of Wesley College, I shall never forget my feelings as I uttered a prayer for God to make me worthy of my father's trust and confidence. They were hard but happy years that I spent in the university. I passed the Oxford University entrance tests and later mastered my preliminary law examination. Two years after that came the very hard intermediate law examination which I managed to get through and then came the end of college days. It was during these years that I first commenced to drift. While I loved my parents deeply, I foolishly began to believe that their outlook on life was old-fashioned and rather narrow. I had been caught in a social whirl and had become the friend of the sons of men, some of them titled, who lived in a very different sphere from my simple and beautiful home surroundings. Down again went my father into his pocket. I was articled to a celebrated Sheffield law firm. At first I was fascinated by the atmosphere of the court rooms and the pleading of the barristers in criminal cases and I enjoyed preparing briefs. I came in contact with such a moving, restless tide of humanity. How well do I remember the endless grist of broken lives that went through the mills of British judicial procedure. Sometimes they haunted me. After awhile I became more and more restless. Strange are the circumstances of life that sometimes pick you up like a mighty cyclone, and, whirling you around until you hardly know where you are, set you down at last in some far distant place. Thus it was I found myself in Canada.

3
IN CANADA

I have given you a somewhat detailed account of the background of my life and the early days of my boyhood because I think these things played a very important part in the things that were to come afterwards. How mysteriously and wonderfully God moves! Was the hand of the Lord in it all? Did He see the end from the beginning? Would I ever have come in contact with the full Gospel had I never left old England? These are some questions that can only be answered when the light of eternity beams upon them. In my heart I know that God has led, directed and guided me even in the days when I did not know Him.

"This my song through countless ages:
    Jesus led me all the way."

In vain did I search for employment in the law offices of Canada. From Quebec to Winnipeg I visited scores and scores of lawyers, but none of them seemed to have any opening for the green young fellow just away from England. I have not time to tell you of the struggle and privations of those early days. I was down to my last dollar when I shipped out of Winnipeg on a cattle train. I slept in the same car as the bellowing herd, and while the train rolled across the vast prairies of Canada I could not help but contrast my position then with my school and home life back in the old country.

I arrived ultimately at Medicine Hat. There I was given a home by some old friends of my parents, who had emigrated to Canada some years before. Mr. Simpson was a car repairer for the Canadian Pacific Railway. He had been a boyhood friend of my father. Mrs. Simpson had helped my mother make her wedding dress, and had held me on her lap when I was just a few hours old. She had not seen me for eighteen or nineteen years, and I shall never forget her expression of amazement when I told her who I was, as I stood outside her door. They gave me shelter, and I made my home with them for several months.

Through Mr. Simpson's influence, I landed my first job in Canada. I worked on the car repairing tracks, called in the vocabulary of the railroad the "Rip Track." My foreman was a genial Irishman who took great delight in having all the fun he could at my expense and much to the amazement of the rest of the gang. My pay was twenty-one and a half cents an hour and I worked for ten hours every day. During that winter it got bitterly cold. There were nights when the thermometer went to thirty degrees below zero.

Night after night the call boy would rouse me from my bed and I would have to go down to the railroad yards to wait for the trains that had been delayed by the storms. We would huddle around a natural gas fire in a little shack, waiting for the screaming of the locomotive whistle. I can see those great engines now as they came in covered with snow and ice. My task was to climb on top of the coaches and, dragging a heavy hose with me, pound the ice from certain openings so that I could fill the tanks with water. More than once the hose would freeze solid while I was going from one car to another. More than once I slipped and fell while making the jump from coach to coach. Life was a hard struggle, but it was good for me.

A Change

Then came the days when I had to leave Medicine Hat. Sickness in the home made it impossible for them to care for me any more. They insisted on my staying, and if I had remained in the town I knew I could not stay at any other place, for it would have wounded the feelings of my dear friends. But I knew that the dear old motherly soul could not stand the work my presence made necessary.

One night I was sitting with an open map before me. A strange feeling came upon me. I felt impressed to go to Spokane. I did not want to go to the United States. I preferred to stay in the land of the maple leaf. I could not get rid of the feeling, however, that I should go to Spokane.

Whose was the voice that spoke to me? What power was it that was drawing me over the line? Packing my grip I left Medicine Hat, bound for Vancouver. I stopped off at Nelson, British Columbia, and was so fascinated by the beauty of Kootenay Lake that I decided to stay awhile and thought perhaps I would make that place my future home. It was while there that I was awakened in the night, and once again felt that strange and now almost irresistible urge to go to Spokane. In my heart I argued against it, and in my mind I reasoned against it. We shall see why just a little later.

It was quite by accident that I met Mr. Winlaw who was the owner of a great logging camp, situated fifty miles away from Nelson, way up in the mountains. He offered me a job and I took it. Never shall I forget the life I lived in those glorious mountains of British Columbia! I washed dishes—I peeled potatoes —I went out with the swamping crew and made roads—I handled the chains for the donkey engine crew and learned how to manipulate a cant hook by the side of the narrow gauge railroad. I worked on the log booms down at the place where the huge pieces of timber rolled into the waters of the lake. It was hard but it was fascinating work. The clean smell of the pine needle forest was wonderful to me. In my spare time I would wander through the virgin woods, glimpsing the wild life with which the countryside abounded. I borrowed a rifle and started to hunt, and more than once brought in game to be used as food for the camp.

Lonely

But in my heart I was lonely. I wondered about my father's new home on the sloping hillside above Hope valley in Derbyshire. It was a beautiful place. From a barefoot boy by the side of his father's forge, my father had made his way until he was now living the life of a retired gentleman in a lovely country home. Sitting there among the trees in British Columbia, I would think of the garden my father's labor had made. I would dream of the rolling river, old Derwent Water, that rippled past the stepping stones—and wonder what they were doing in the old home while I was far away.

One night I was sitting by the dying embers of a camp fire. In one of the nearby shacks a group of loggers were making crude harmony. As they were singing together and playing stringed instruments (whatever started them doing it I do not know) suddenly the strains of "Beulah Land" came floating into my ear. It was one of my father's favorite songs. As I gazed into the fire—transfixed—the tears suddenly burst from my eyes. I could hear him sing just as if he were close by my side:

O Beulah Land, sweet Beulah Land,
As on the highest mount I stand,
I look away across the sea,
Where mansions are prepared for me,
And view the shining glory shore;
My heaven, my home for evermore!

I struggled for a few moments with my emotions and then slowly and tearfully walked to my shack and bunk. Just as I was dropping off to sleep again that mysterious voice spoke to me, "Spokane! Spokane!" For an hour or two I tossed restlessly and then made a resolution. Suddenly a peace came over me and I fell asleep. The following day I left for Spokane.

4
MY EARLY MINISTRY

A few months passed by. One night, in the early autumn, I was standing with my back against a lamp post listening to the singing of a little band of mission workers. They gave testimony after testimony and then invited the hearers to go into the mission hall, where an evening service was to be held. They pointed across the street to where the words "Life Line Mission" stood out brilliantly upon the painted window. A tiny, white-haired old lady had been playing the little, portable organ. Every time I glanced her way, I found her gazing intently at me. I wondered who she was and why she seemed to be so interested in me. Looking cautiously her way once again our eyes met. She smiled at me and I raised my hat and smiled back.

When the street meeting was over I started to walk away, but the dear old soul detained me. Looking into my eyes she said, "Do you believe in the Lord?" "Oh yes," I said, "Of course I do. I come from a real Christian home." She looked at me very kindly and said, "I thought you did. As a matter of fact, I knew you did. Do you know that God wants you?" I looked at her in amazement. "God wants me," I said, "for what purpose and how do you know that?"

"While I was playing the organ tonight," she replied, "the Lord spoke to my heart by His Spirit and told me that He wanted you. You must come to the mission. You must attend the service tonight. It seems as if I cannot let you go." Suddenly I felt uncomfortable. I am afraid I was rather rude in the way I excused myself and hurried away. I walked as fast as I could out to the Monroe Street bridge, but half way across the bridge, I stopped. A peculiar feeling came over me, and a voice that was not a voice seemed to be talking to me. I began to feel as if God might have spoken to the old lady, and a feeling akin to dread and awe came upon me. Slowly I retraced my steps and arrived eventually at the mission. I sat in the very back and listened to the preaching of the Superintendent, Rev. E. H. Stayt.

A big Norwegian was sitting next to me, dressed in the clothes of a lumber jack. I pulled his sleeve and said, "Who is that little old lady that is looking this way? Do you know her?" "Yes," he replied, "that is Mother Walker." "She looks like a kind little old woman," I said. The Norwegian looked down at me and said, "She isn't no old woman, she is the nearest thing to an angel I have ever seen." Little did I know that in days to come I was to preach and work with her in jails and in hospitals, on the street corner, and in the mission as the Lord Himself would open the door. Dear old Mother Walker, dear saint of God, has long since gone to the reward of them that love the Lord.

Saved

What a battle went on in my heart that night! The road I was going led down. I knew it. Bitterness had crept into my heart. I was getting to the place where I did not care what happened, and while I was not in the gutter, yet I was slipping down, down, down, and I knew it was disaster and sorrow in the end. When Mr. Stayt gave his altar call, I sprang to my feet, squared my shoulders and marched down to the front. In a moment I felt a hand on my shoulder. It was very light and gentle. I turned around and there looking at me was the smiling face of Mother Walker. "I knew you would come back," she whispered. "I wasn't a bit afraid. The Lord told you to come, didn't He?" I had to admit that He did.

That night I gave myself to God. I was desperately in earnest. I was absolutely sincere. I did not have, however, the great emotional experience that came to me in an event that I shall describe later. It was a quiet, methodical, almost business-like proposition I made to the Lord; yet I meant it. I was sincere. Mr. Stayt gave me his hand, when I stepped to my feet and said, "Would you not like to testify?" So I did. There were no tears, no surging of emotion, but just a plain matter-of-fact statement that I had given myself to God and from that time on would live a Christian life. With all my heart I meant it.

The next night I was on the street and gave my testimony. During the opening of the service, I followed the little band into the hall and gave my testimony once again. From that time on, I was a regular attendant and never missed a night's service in the old mission. Winter came and with it the cold snowy nights. One dark and very stormy night, I made my way through the gale to the old "Life Line Mission." Very few were there and we decided it would be impossible to hold a street meeting, for it was snowing and was bitterly cold.

We built a huge fire and soon had the

building cozy and warm. One by one people commenced to come in. Most of them were men who were anxious to find shelter from the bitter, biting blast of the winter's night. The hour for service had come and Mr. Stayt had not arrived. A few of the mission workers were insistent that I take charge of the service. I hesitated and then said that I would try. It was not so bad leading the song service, but when it came time to preach my knees knocked together. Just as I was giving out my text, "If a man have an hundred sheep, and one of them be gone astray, doth he not leave the ninety and nine, and go into the mountains, and seek that which is gone astray?" the door opened and a gentleman came in who seemed to stand out from the rest of the crowd. He kept nodding encouragement to me. The end of the message came and I gave an altar call. Two men knelt and found their Savior that night.

"God Wants You"

After the benediction was pronounced, the well-dressed gentleman came from the back of the building and grasped my hand. "What is the name?" he enquired. I told him. "How long have you been preaching here?" he said. I told him that that was the first time I had ever preached a sermon in all my life. He asked about my schooling, my family, my work. Then he put his arm around me and said, "My boy, God wants you. I believe He led me into this mission tonight to speak to you. My name is Henry I. Rasmus. I am pastor of the First Methodist Church here in Spokane. You are going to become a Methodist preacher. I want to meet you tomorrow morning at ten o'clock in my study. Do not forget what I have told you. I believe with all my heart that God wants you."

That night I did not sleep. The following morning I knelt in the study of Dr. Henry I. Rasmus, who putting his hand on my head, asked God to take charge of my life. The Life

Line Mission was a Free Methodist Mission and taught and practiced the old-fashioned Wesleyan doctrine of scriptural holiness. They were wonderful people and they lived very, very close to God. Very soon after my decision to enter the ministry had been reached I became a paid worker in this mission and for a while assumed the superintendency.

I went out as a representative of the mission work to many of the nearby cities. My meetings were generally held in Methodist churches that opened their doors to me largely through the influence of Dr. Rasmus, and I was introduced to the Superintendent of the Methodist Church, called in those days, Presiding Elder. He promised me a local pastorate after he had brought the matter before the annual conference.

Just about this time I was married and, having received a letter from a friend in Seattle, I moved with my young bride to that city on Puget Sound. Having worked in a Free Methodist Mission, I soon became acquainted with the Free Methodist people in the City of Seattle. The District Superintendent promised me a supply pulpit within the next few months if I could only wait.

First Pastorate

At that particular time, work was very scarce and I had responsibilities of married life now, so I felt I must needs take the first thing that came to hand. I saw an advertisement in the paper, stating that one of the largest grocery firms in Seattle, and certainly the most exclusive, needed a candy maker. I had never made a piece of candy in my life, but believe it or not, I landed the job. I was frank with my new employers, kept my eyes and ears open, and before very long was making huge caldrons of caramels of every kind and shape. I became quite an expert in the manufacture of creams for chocolate centers. Then my presiding elder came to see me and told me the opening was ready.

My first church was at Sedro-Wooley,

Washington. I do not think it would hold more than fifty people. I lived in a tiny house a few blocks away from the church, but felt quite important in my new duties as pastor. My salary was twenty-five to thirty dollars a month, some of which was paid in lettuce, cabbage and celery; while every once in a while someone would bring in a piece of meat. From there we went to Anacortes, where I was pastor of the Free Methodist church. There I spent two very happy years.

During my stay in Anacortes, I held some fairly large meetings, renting the Moose Hall and attracting so much attention with the "clean-up crusade" that even the Seattle papers took notice of the campaign. A series of circumstances took me back to the Inland Empire, arid I found myself once again in Spokane, Mr. Rasmus welcomed me home and immediately got me in touch with the presiding elder, Mr. Luce, who sent me to Athol, Idaho, as a supply pastor.

Ordained

Events moved swiftly now. I was admitted to the conference and ordained by Bishop Smith. Slowly but surely I commenced to get bigger and bigger appointments from my Bishop. I built two parsonages, used all my benevolences, and prided myself on the result of my church ministry. Then something happened. As I look back upon those days I can see how tragic it all was. For you to understand it thoroughly I shall have to go back and describe to you an event that occurred a few years before.

While I was in the Life Line Mission news came of the falling of the power of the Holy Ghost in the City of Los Angeles. One of our mission workers, who was very hungry for God, had gone down to Los Angeles and received what she called the "baptism of the Holy Spirit." Before her return, a fiery evangelist had come up from California and had rented a large building not very far from where my mission was situated. He came to see me. He poured out his heart, as he told me of the falling of the old-time power. He told of miracles of healing. He spoke in convincing terms of the latter days and the soon return of the Lord.

I promised him that I would go home and pray. I did, and slowly conviction came over my soul. Then to add to it, two of my mission workers came to see me and joyously proclaimed they were different men—their faces were different—their eyes blazed with the glory that was heavenly and there was power and conviction in their testimony. I promised to meet them at a certain time and place the following day so that they might pray for me that I might be filled with the Holy Ghost. When I went home I was walking on air.

5
THE TWO ROADS

On my way to the prayer meeting the next day, I met a certain minister. He asked me down to his home. I told him I could not come for I was on my way to a prayer meeting. He asked me what kind of a prayer meeting it was I was attending at that hour of the day. I enthusiastically explained the whole situation to him. To my amazement he gripped me by the arm and said, "Price, I cannot let you go. You will wreck your future —your life. You are young and inexperienced. If you take this step, you will regret it as long as you live." Listening to his voice I yielded. He pleaded for the chance to show me wherein these people were all wrong.

All afternoon I sat with him in his study and when I left he had given me half a suitcase full of books that I promised to read. I did not go to the prayer meeting. That was the turning point in my life. With all my heart I believe that God had led me to Spokane so that I might step through the open door into the glorious experience I am enjoying today, but I listened to the voice of a modernist and by my own act closed the door. Two roads were opened before me and I took the wrong one. I foolishly turned my back on the cross and started along the trail that led to the labyrinth of modernism.

Greater battles have been fought on the battle field of the human soul than ever raged at Thermopylae (Spartans), Waterloo or Bull Run. The conflict within my own breast was the age-old battle of reason against faith. How grieved and sorry I am today to have to record that reason won.

I very soon got to checkpoint where I could explain every religious emotion from the standpoint of psychology. I argued that a man's belief would affect his feeling even though he was in error regarding the thing he believed. I argued that when reason did not reign as king then one was ruled entirely by feeling and emotion, and how unreliable these things really were!

The result of it all was that I drifted down the long highway that led me into modernism. I never gave an altar call—never led a soul to Jesus—never preached the glory of a born-again experience——but just simply preached for the love of preaching in an endeavor to influence the lives of my congregation toward "the right." I can truthfully say that there was no hypocrisy in my ministry. I preached what I believed and believed what I preached, but just the same I was spiritually blind, leading my people into the ditch.

Broader Fields

The years marched swiftly by. Methodist pastorate followed pastorate, most of them being in northern Idaho and the eastern part of Washington. I was a member of the Columbia River Conference of the Methodist Church. Slowly and surely I was climbing the rungs of the ladder to what my ministerial brethren called success. I began to be in demand as a speaker in churches throughout the countryside. I commenced to emphasize the social ethics of Jesus. How my heart grieves when I contemplate those days that might have been filled with so much of good for God and yet after all, they were so empty.

After a while I reached the place where my godly, presiding elder had to take me to task for some of my modernistic utterances. I began to feel the restraining, binding influence of the Methodist Episcopal System. I believed that if only I could get a congregation that would not be amenable to any higher authority than myself, then I could influence and mold that congregation into what I thought a church should be. Week in and week out the struggle continued in my heart. I spent a whole afternoon in the office of an official of the Congregational church, and when eventually I left that office, I had made up my mind to sever my connection with Methodism and branch out into the "broader" field that the Congregational church offered me.

Thus it was I became the pastor of the Congregational church at Valdez, Alaska, and superintendent of the Congregational missions in that part of the territory. With my family, I moved up to the quaint little mining town situated on the flats at the foot of the great Valdez Glacier.

The land of the great white silence fascinated me. I soon acquired a dog team, one of the very best in that part of the country, and became expert in the driving of my dogs. I have slept out on the snows with my team around me when there was not a house within miles and when nothing could be heard in the clear cold of the arctic night but the plaintive howling of the wolves.

I hunted for wild game in the best, wild game fields of the world. I stalked the Kodiak bear on Kodiak Island and hunted sheep in the mountains that border the Matanuska. I photographed the great fur seal herds on the Pribilof Islands in the heart of the Bering Sea, and mushed my way across Alaska from Cook's Inlet to Bristol Bay. What thrilling days they were! Full of adventure and excitement.

How well I can remember my first climb into the mountains that overlook the "valley of a thousand smokes." How well I can feel the rumbling now of the ground beneath my feet as I saw old Katmai belching forth its smoke and its fire! I saw the walrus herds playing on the ice floes and watched the silver horde of salmon running up the rivers that empty into the Bering Sea—a great silvery horde of fish that shone in the sunlight like a million diamonds on the surface of the water. I hunted whales from a whaling vessel and in the winter walked with my snow-shoes over snow that in some places was sixty feet deep. I loved Alaska—the thrill of it—the challenge of it—the excitement of it!

Alaskan Floating Court

It was while I was there that I was made a member of the United States Alaskan Floating Court. The reason for the court was that the distances in Alaska are so vast and the means of transportation so limited that it was impossible for the prisoners to be brought to the court town of Valdez for trial, so the court went annually to them. I was made the chaplain also of the most northerly lodge of the Order of the Eastern Star in the world. I was quite prominent in Masonic work. I joined the Arctic Brotherhood and the Sourdough Association. Illness in my family, however, compelled me to leave the north; and I shall never forget the unhappy day when I had to sell my faithful dogs and board the steamer that brought me back to the United States.

Santa Rosa

I landed in San Francisco and immediately

set to work arranging the pictures, thousands of them, that I had taken of the wild and native life of Alaska. I soon accepted a call to the First Congregational Church of Santa Rosa and while there I became very well acquainted with Luther Burbank, the wizard of the botanical world.

During my pastorate there I decided to organize what was called in religious circles, an "Institutional Church." The mayor of the city assisted in the dedication and when it was all over, the doors of the Sunday School rooms and class-rooms were thrown open every night of the week to men who wanted to come in and play billiards, pool and many other kinds of games. My idea was to elevate the man on the street to the level of the church. It did not work. I knew before it had been running six months that it was a failure, but absolutely refused to admit it.

The members of the church were splendid people, loyal and liberal, and gave me their finest cooperation. Then came the call from the Calvary Church of Oakland, California. I accepted and moved down to the civic life in which I was destined to play for a while quite a prominent part. I would give everything in the world to have the opportunity to live those days over again.

I became a popular type of preacher. I was appointed a "Four-Minute Man" and used to speak from every theater stage in the city. It was, of course, during the terrible days of the World War. My work brought me a letter from Woodrow Wilson, then President of the United States, and an appointment as a member of the United States Committee on Public Information. I joined the Lion's Club and also belonged to five fraternal organizations.

When the government organized the local Liberty Loan Committee, I was made a member of it. When the great motion picture stars came to help in the war drives, I was generally chosen as the principal speaker of the evening, for very few of them made any attempt to talk above a few minutes. They used the motion-picture stars to draw the crowds and used me to sell the bonds. I am sorry to say that I attained such popularity that at the close of the war many of the theaters in San Francisco and Oakland solicited my services. Their terms were so generous and my church board offering no objection I accepted their offers. For many months I was on the stage during the week and in the pulpit on Sunday. I want to confess that my heart was heavy; and behind all of my jokes and wise-cracking before the audiences in the theaters, there was a great big ache deep down in the depths of my being. Oh, if I had only gone to that Holy Ghost prayer meeting years before in the city of Spokane, how different my life would have been!

Chautauqua Lecturing

Next came a contract from the Ellison-White Chautauqua System. Their first contract called for fifteen consecutive weeks with my two illustrated lectures. "Hunting Big Game in Alaska" and "With the Floating

Court to the Pribilof Islands." This was followed by Lyceum work. An assistant pastor was employed by my church so that I might have time to get into what I called my broader field of the lecture platform. Then I moved to Lodi, a beautiful town in Northern California and the center of the Tokay grape industry, where I was pastor of the First Congregational Church. It was a wonderful church with wonderful people.

Never shall I forget as long as I live the big hearts and kindnesses of the people of that church. Sickness came into my home and when my own funds were all gone in battling it the church loyally took up the burden and gave me more than I needed. I was presented with two automobiles while there, and greatly enjoyed my pastorate. I gave up a great deal of my outside work, although I did keep on with Chautauqua lecturing, and the church was generally packed to the doors. Quite often on week nights I would give illustrated lectures of my experiences in various parts of the world. Then something happened. I come

now to the part of the story that I love to tell
the most.

6
LIGHT FROM HEAVEN

It all began when a good brother came running across the lawn outside the parsonage to meet me one certain summer day. His eyes were fairly dancing and on his face was the joy of heaven itself. Clasping my hand he said, "Brother Price—Hallelujah!—Hallelujah!—Praise the Lord!" I gazed at him in amazement. Expressions like that were not usual in my church. We were like the majority of churches, rather cold and formal. Throwing back my head, I commenced to laugh. "Where in the world have you been?" I asked. Still clasping my hand, he said, "Hallelujah—I have been to San Jose and I have been saved—saved—through the blood.

I am so happy that I could just float away."

It amused me. The more I ridiculed him, however, the more vehement he became in his testimony. I then discovered that some more of the members of my church had contacted that meeting and were loud in their praises unto God. Slowly a bitter antagonism commenced to creep into my heart. They told me of a great campaign where thousands were being saved and thousands were being healed. I answered with my explanation of "mob psychology" and "mental and physical reactions."

Then one day another dear man came along. His was the hand that really first opened the door through which I started into the experience God has given me by His grace and that I enjoy today. His name was A.B. Forrester. Little did I dream when he talked to me that day, that God was using him and his deep sincerity in speaking to my heart; but still I rebelled—was openly antagonistic. It was the influence of Mr. Forrester that got me to change my mind. I agreed that I would attend the meetings, after I had said I never would go.

Inserting an advertisement in the paper that I would preach the following Sunday on "Divine Healing Bubble Explodes," I made my way down to San Jose, armed with pen and paper to take notes. I intended to return the following Sunday and blow the whole thing to pieces. That was my frame of mind. My automobile rolled over the hundred miles that separated my home town from San Jose and as I neared the city a peculiar feeling came over my heart. Across the street was a huge sign in startling, flashing letters, "Aimee Semple-McPherson; auspices "William Keeny Towner."

I could hardly believe my eyes. Dr. Towner had been pastor of the First Baptist Church in Oakland during the time that I was pastor at Calvary Church. We had been friends and more than once I had seen him laughing at me as I was on the theater stage and on more than one occasion we had gone into the theater together. He was a splendid man, noble and kind, but I knew he was not the type of preacher to back an old-fashioned Holy Ghost revival meeting. I thought that he must be getting something out of it or that he had done it to carry out some policy.

Going to the very edge of town, I found the huge tent seating approximately six thousand people. To my utter amazement it was packed and a great crowd was standing around the outside. The afternoon service was just over. Elbowing my way through and pushing myself toward a place I could see, I noticed that the platform was empty. There was seemingly no program to hold the people. A tall, gaunt man stood by my side. I looked up into his face and said, "Pardon me, sir. What are all these people waiting for?" He looked at me and then suddenly his face broke into a big grin and he literally shouted, "Hallelujah!—Praise the Lord!—They are waiting for the evening service."

Questionings

I smiled back at him and said, "Well, that 'Hallelujah' business seems to be pretty general around here. It must be catching I suppose. Something like the measles."

His hand came down on my shoulder until he got a grip like a vice and then he said, "This is a good place to get the 'Hallelujahs,' my friend. You stick around here and the Lord will get you sure."

I glanced down the aisle. Walking up toward me I saw my old friend, Dr. Towner. Standing on my tip-toes and waving my hand, I called across, "Bill, oh there, Bill!" We were intimate enough to call each other by our given names. His dear face broke into a wreath of smiles. Rushing over to me he grabbed my hand. "Charlie Price," he said, "Well, Hallelujah!—Glory to Jesus!—Praise the Lord!"

My jaw dropped. A look of amazement came over my face.

"W-well what—?" I exclaimed, "have you

got them too?"

"Got what?" he inquired.

"Why, the 'Hallelujahs,'" I declared.

"Yes," he said, "I have got the 'Hallelujahs' and a whole lot more." As he spoke a peculiar feeling seized my heart. I wanted to know more of this matter, so taking hold of his arm I pulled him through the crowd. When we were all alone I said to him, "Come on, now, be honest with me, tell me all about it. What are you getting out of it and what is all this 'Hallelujah' business about?"

Looking into my eyes with a serious expression, he said, "Charlie, this is real. This little woman is right. This is the real Gospel. I have been baptized with the Holy Ghost. It is genuine, I tell you. It is what you need."

In amazement I gazed at him. Then I said, "Do you mean to tell me that you, one of the leading Baptist preachers in the West—William Keeny Towner—have actually swallowed this stuff?"

His eyes twinkled. "Charles," he said, "I have swallowed the pole, line, reel, hook, bait and sinker—and yet I am so hungry, I am looking around for some more."

Shouting "Thank God for the Baptism," he shook my hand and left me, promising to see me later. Pushing my way back through the crowd to get a place where I could see, I accidentally stepped upon a man's toe. I looked up into his face and said, "I beg your pardon."

He smiled back and said, "Hallelujah."

"I expected that," I declared, and kept on going. Praises unto God were certainly in order around that tent. Once again in an advantageous position, I looked over the crowd. Why, there was Ole, my old Swedish usher! During Chautauqua days I was forced to remonstrate with him because of his dirty habit of chewing Copenhagen snuff. Ole looked different to me. He was cleaner and there were no dark corners around his mouth.

He displayed a big red badge and said, "Hallelujah! Praise the Lord Yesus! I ban an oosher."

Mischievously I said, "Where is the snuff,

Ole?" Back he came at me with "Hallelujah, I ban saved; I ban healed; I ban filled with the Holy Ghost; I ban so full with glory there ain't any room for snoos."

His testimony brought a little cry of "Hallelujahs" and "Praise the Lords" from the people around, much to my embarrassment. The folks in the crowd were beginning to look in our direction. I asked Ole to find me a seat. I promised him to stand where I was and he went in search of one for me. Ten minutes later he came back.

"What a yob!" he said, "what a yob! But I ban got one for you."

I followed him down the aisle and, to my amazement and added embarrassment, he led me to the very front, then swinging around like a soldier, he led me all the way across the long altar, then suddenly swinging into another left turn he pointed out a chair that was empty in the section reserved for cripples. That is where I belonged, but I did not know it at that time. I was crippled in a different place than they were. All the way down the aisle I could hear people mentioning my name. My face turned red. One very good sister said in a very audible tone of voice, "Praise the Lord, here comes Dr. Price. I hope he gets something." I did, but that is another part of the story.

7
MY CONVERSION

It was not the sermon that convinced me that night, half so much as the altar call. The altars were literally filled with people. It had been years and years and years since I had seen anything like that and never in all my life had I beheld so many people kneeling at one time before their Lord. They put chairs in the aisles to accommodate the seekers. A man came to kneel by the chair next to mine. He was a garage mechanic. I knew him well. He was a wonderful worker, but a man of oaths and blasphemy. I could not help but hear him pray.

Suddenly, in the midst of his intercession, a great change came over his face. Jumping to his feet, he shouted, "Glory!" Lifting his hands in the air, he commenced praising God. Then he opened his eyes. I was the first man he saw and I presume he thought that being a minister I ought to rejoice with him in the salvation he had found. At the very top of his lungs he shouted, "Hallelujah, I am saved. Isn't it wonderful? Isn't it glorious, Mr. Price?"

I tried to conceal my embarrassment because of the noise he was making and the emotion he was showing. The best I could do was to say, "Yes, brother, stick to it, stick to it"—and I got out of the tent as fast as I could. I did not sleep that night. In spirit, I was back in my old English home. In fancy, I was crossing again the prairies of Canada. In imagination, I was behind the pulpit in the Life Line Mission. Deep down in my heart, something told me that in recent years I had been wrong—not insincere, but wrong. That is why I tossed restlessly through the long night watches and no sleep came to give me relief.

The next night a masterful message came

from the lips of the evangelist and my modernistic theology was punctured until it looked like a sieve. Arriving at my hotel room, I threw myself down on my knees and cried out to God. The heavens were black above me and no answer came; yet, in the sincerity of my heart, I promised God that I would change. I told Him I would preach the old-time Gospel, if only He would bless me and reveal Himself to me. Oh, the agony of those moments! The intensity of those prayers! In my heart, I wanted the change to be gradual. I was afraid the members of the church might think I had been hypocritical and insincere. God wanted it otherwise and I am glad today He closed the gates of heaven to my pleas that night. He had a far more excellent way!

Reclaimed

The following night I went early to the meeting. The place was crowded and I could not find a seat. Dr. Towner saw me wandering around, and slipping his arm affectionately around me said, "Charles, why do you not come to the platform? There is nothing to be ashamed of. Let us sit together tonight and enjoy the service."

Up to that time I had refused to go near the platform, although I had been invited on two occasions. I promised him that I would go if he could find seats at the back. We discovered two but when we went to sit in them we found Bibles there, showing that they belonged to someone else. Having gone on to the platform I could not very well leave it.

That would make me too conspicuous. So I had to sit in the front row.

How marvelously that great audience sang! How wonderfully the great choir thundered out, "There Is Power, Power, Wonder-Working Power in the Blood of the Lamb"! Every time they said the word "Power," it was like the blow of a mighty hammer upon an anvil such as my grandfather used to wield by his forge in old England so far away. All during the opening part of the service I was conscious of God speaking to my heart. Then came the sermon. It was preached for me. Halfway through the message I had made up my mind what I was going to do and I kept praying to God for strength to carry out my resolution.

The message was over. It was the moment of the altar call. I can hear her now as she said, "I want every man and woman in this audience who will say, 'Sister, I am a sinner; I need Jesus and I want you to pray for me,' to stand to your feet." Tremblingly I stood. A hand was put on my shoulder and the voice of a prominent Presbyterian minister sounded in my ear, "Charles, she is calling for sinners. She is calling for people who need to be saved." I whispered back "I know it," and I kept on standing. Then came the rest of the invitation. "Come down and kneel before the Lord. Come ye weary and heavy laden and He will give you rest."

Down those steps I walked. I was in the act of kneeling at the altar when the glory of God broke over my soul. I did not pray for I did not have to pray. Something burst within my breast. An ocean of love divine rolled across my heart. This was out of the range of psychology and actions and reactions. This was real!! Throwing up both hands I shouted, "Hallelujah!" So overcome was I with joy that I commenced to run across the altar. Dr. Towner followed me—and wept for joy! Then in an ecstasy of divine glory I ran down the aisle to the back of the tent and back to the front again, shouting, "I am saved— Hallelujah!—I am saved!"

My Heart Afire

God was answering the prayer of a mother who had prayed many, many years before in a little English home. That night the hand with the nail-print in it guided me out onto a new road that would inspire me to preach the Gospel to millions of people and send the printed Word to practically every country in the world. After the great tent had been emptied that night—I went back to pray. It was so dark and silent—but I was rejoicing in the light in my heart. A half hour passed—and then I stood to my feet. "Oh Christ," I sobbed, "where You lead me, I will follow—I mean it—I mean it—only go Thou with me all the way." In the deep, deep center of my being, I was conscious of His presence. As I walked out into the cool night air He whispered, "Fear not, for I have redeemed thee. I have called thee by thy name—thou art Mine."

In the course of a few days not only my viewpoint and outlook on life, but my life itself had been transformed and changed. The burning, flaming fires of evangelism began to blaze in my heart. The thing that I desired more than anything else in the world was to win souls for Jesus. Through the corridors of my mind there marched the heralds of Divine truth carrying their banners on which I could see emblazoned: "Jesus Saves," "Heaven Is Real," "Christ Lives Today," until my whole heart became filled with the glory of His Presence Divine. I was also conscious of the fact that these people with whom I had come in contact had an experience that I did not possess. There was an indescribable something about their testimony, their prayers, their preaching, that I lacked, even though I was filled with the joy of the Lord. What was it? Was it the baptism of the Holy Spirit that the evangelist had spoken about in Spokane so many years before? Was it that experience that the Lord had brought me all the way down from Medicine Hat to receive but that I had rejected when I allowed a minister to influence my young life?

Was God giving me a second chance? I must confess to you when I commenced to reason it out even then, I felt I could never go into the tarrying room to wait for the enduement with power. All reason, all logic, all my own interpretation of Scripture, all my old training and theology was against it. In desperation I cried out unto the Lord. Hands raised toward heaven I prayed for kindly light that would lead me through the gloom. The light came. The Lord who sent light through the darkness to Saul on the Damascus road did not refuse me. It was in my study at home, by the side of my desk, alone with God in the early hours of the morning that I made my decision.

8
FILLED WITH THE SPIRIT

I went back to San Jose. Arriving there, I immediately hunted up my old friend, Dr. Towner, and told him my story. He informed me that they were holding meetings every night called "tarrying meetings," for the specific purpose of waiting before God so that men and women might be filled with the Holy Ghost.

I wanted power—power—power. Old-time power. Holy Ghost power. Power to pray. Power to preach. Power to lead sinful men and women to the foot of the old rugged cross.

So night after night found me tarrying in the Baptist church. How tenderly God dealt with me. How sweetly He led me, step by step, nearer and nearer to the glorious Baptism. Hallelujah! I have to shout when I think about it. I get so happy I want to be baptized all over again.

Some things did bother me. The noise, for instance. Why did people get so noisy? Why could they not pray quietly and with a dignity to which I had been accustomed? Why did they—Oh, why did they fall over in such undignified postures? They were under the power of God all over the building. The church was filled; the Sunday school room was filled; the vestries were filled; and they were even praying in the kitchen.

Happy Night

Then came a glorious night. Shall I ever forget it? Never—not in time and not in eternity! Hallelujah! On this night—happy night, oh, happy night—there was no room for me to pray in the church, so I made my way into the Sunday school room, and I found it crowded, too. Everybody was praying. I looked at them, and then I looked at myself, in my long-tailed Prince Albert coat, and wondered why it was necessary for God to straighten people out on their backs like that.

I didn't think it was necessary. I said to Dr. Towner: "Do I have to go down?"

He said: "Yes."

And I said: "You told somebody else he didn't have to."

"It's this way, Charlie, YOU DON'T WANT TO, and therefore YOU WILL HAVE TO."

I said: "Suppose I should tell the Lord I want to." He said: "He wouldn't believe you. You should be willing to let go and let Him have His way."

I saw so many people under the power I began to be bothered again about that undignified position for a Congregational minister. I noticed the piano. There was a little space back of it and it made a little private room. When I thought I would not attract any attention, I got back of the piano and took

69

the piano stool with me. I had room enough to kneel, but not room to fall over.

I started to pray and I prayed and prayed until I had lost all sense of time. About one o'clock in the morning Dr. Towner came along with two deacons and started moving the piano. He looked at me and said:

"What are you doing here?"

I said, "I am praying."

He got hold of the tail of my coat with one hand and the back of my head with the other and said, "There's too much of this and too much of this"

I said, "I know what you mean." I felt so small!

Dr. Towner said, "Why don't you get out in the middle of the room, where the power is falling? Get where God is blessing people." I got in the middle of the room and there saw one of my parishioners under the power. The glory of God was upon her, shaking her from head to foot. As I looked at her, I said, "That's real"; and got on my knees with my elbows resting on a chair. I must have prayed for a few minutes when I heard them singing: "Have Thine Own Way, Lord." "Yes, Lord, I have come to the place where I can say, 'Have Thine Own Way.' If you want to put me on my back in the middle of the street, Amen!"

Visions

Dr. Towner evidently decided I was getting in real earnest, so he started to pray. I raised my hands. That was the first time I had done that, and I commenced to look up with my eyes closed. When my hands were up for a little while I felt an electrical feeling starting down my fingers and when it got to my arms, my hands commenced to tingle and I looked at them and there they were shaking. I was surprised. I couldn't have stopped if I had wanted to, and I wouldn't resist the Spirit. I said: "All right, Lord." And by the time the glory waves got to my head, my head commenced to shake. Then, down it came to my body, glorious, wonderful power and suddenly I got a real bolt of glory. I felt myself suddenly going up; but I found I wasn't going up, I was going down: Prince Albert and everything, down on the floor. I commenced to praise God. Did you ever watch the waves of the ocean as they break and roll and break? Just a wave that breaks and then rolls back, and then another wave? Dr. Towner, who was praying to the Lord, by my side, cried unto Him saying, "Give him more."

But I said, "Brother Towner, if I get any more it will kill me."

He said, "Amen! Kill him, Lord."

I didn't understand that then, but I did later. He told me afterwards THAT WAS WHAT I NEEDED. The dear old preacher kept praising and praying, and after about twenty minutes of that, I sank into the depths of an infinite peace. I quietly praised the Lord. At that moment a woman put her hand on me and Dr. Towner said, "Don't do that. Leave him with God."

With my eyes closed, I seemed to be looking up into the dark. Suddenly like a knife, there appeared in that awful dark a light and it flashed like a lightning flash across the blackness above my head. The heavens were split and they commenced to fold up until I could see the glory of a light through that opening in the sky. As I gazed at that beautiful light, a ball of fire came down towards me; lower and lower it came until it got to the level of the darkness on either side. It began to shoot out darts of fire. Then the ball came down a little lower. It shone so brightly it banished the darkness. After the darkness had been dispelled it hung there for about five minutes. I just watched, fascinated and entranced, those tongues of fire. Then the ball started down again and when it got right above my head, I don't know how high, I remember the fire kept coming out faster and faster until the ball split and a tongue came straight down at me. Dr. Towner said, and the people around me corroborated, that from my lying position, I jumped instinctively to get out of the way of the fire that was going to strike me. I didn't have time to think what it was. It touched me on the forehead and I felt a quiver go through my body and then my chest began to heave and I started praising God. So great was the heaving of my chest that I actually thought my skin had been torn—a burning, and yet no pain. Then suddenly He came. The Comforter arrived. It was so glorious! I knew it the moment He came in. I felt Him come. I started to say: "Glory," but my tongue wouldn't form the word. It was wobbling around in my mouth and I was unable to control it, as I was trying to say: "Glory."

Dr. Towner said, "Don't resist. Let Him have His way."

The Comforter

After a moment I stammered out a few strange mutterings and then—Oh, glory to God, the Spirit Himself took complete control. I knew every word I said. I was speaking in a language I had never known before. Yet every word was as familiar as my own English. Dr. Towner knelt at my side and interpreted it. They tell me I spoke for thirty minutes, although it seemed but a short space of time. I arose to my feet. I was drunk on the wine of the Holy Ghost. I had lost possession of physical faculties. Down I went! They picked me up again, and I fell the second time. Then they put me in a chair and I sat there preaching Jesus. Then I had a time of weeping. Then I got to my feet again and started around with my hands in the air from two o'clock in the morning until half past four; up and down the aisles, shouting loudly in the Sunday school room and in the church, praising the Lord until the break of day. THE COMFORTER HAD COME!

Back At Lodi

Back I went to my home church at Lodi. The following Sunday morning the place was packed to the doors. The preliminary part of the service was cut short for I was anxious to get to the message. I really expected to be dismissed from my pulpit. I never believed that those dear people, who had been so kind and good to me, would tolerate the type of preaching I was determined to give. I had put my whole life before God upon the altar of consecration and I cared not what should happen to me. To be perfectly frank, I expected to have to open a little mission in the city of San Francisco.

During the time I was waiting upon the Lord for the Blessed Holy Spirit, the Lord had shown me a little mission hall with its plain wooden seats and asked me whether or not I was willing to say goodbye to my ambitions and all of my plans and accept that. With all my heart I cried, "Yes, Lord." I meant it; but the Lord had greater and better plans for me, as we shall see.

So it was I ministered that Sunday morning to the people of my home church. How easy it was to preach! The glory of God flowed like a river, until I could hardly speak for the sobbing of the people. "As long as I am pastor," I said, "you will hear one burning message from this pulpit—Jesus Christ and Him crucified. I shall not refrain from giving you the story of the cross and the saving, cleansing power of the blood of Calvary's Lamb."

At the conclusion of the sermon I gave an altar call. To my amazement over eighty people knelt at that altar. My own church people were hungry for more of God. We commenced to hold meetings and multiplied the number of prayer services. The power of God commenced to fall. The prayer meetings grew from an attendance of one hundred to three hundred and then to five hundred. Climbing still higher, they reached the one thousand mark and the church auditorium and the Sunday school rooms were filled with praying people. Instead of closing at half past nine, as had been our custom before, the meetings would run on until the early hours of the morning.

We were obliged to extend the tarrying meetings out of the church into the home and out-buildings of Mr. A.B. Forrester, the dear brother whose influence had been so greatly felt in my life. People came from neighboring cities. Ministers came from as far distant as one hundred miles regularly to attend those meetings. Among them was the Rev. Eugene Bronson who was at that time pastor of the Methodist Church in San Leandro, about one hundred miles away. At the present time he is Dean of the Southern California Bible School, filled with the Spirit and a mighty man of God. In those meetings hundreds upon hundreds were filled with the Holy Ghost. I greatly doubt that Northern California has ever before or since seen such meetings as we held in Lodi soon after our church received the baptism of the Holy Spirit.

Gospel Team

I then organized the Lodi Gospel Team. It soon grew until it had pretty close to one thousand members. It was organized for the purpose of holding street meetings. Once every week we would meet underneath the

Lodi arch and, led by the Salvation Army band from Stockton, conduct meetings in our own home town. Every Friday night, hundreds and hundreds of people would meet at the church with signs on the backs of their automobiles, reading, "Lodi Gospel Team." A parade would start to some nearby city.

More than once I have seen that parade stretch out over two miles, with automobiles of all kinds and sizes, trucks, etc., carrying a happy singing band of people to testify for the Lord Jesus Christ. I want to remind you that these were Congregational people, whose numbers had been increased by recruits from most of the other churches of the town. We did not proselyte. All we were after was the preaching of the Gospel to the hearts of hungry men.

Spiritual enthusiasm ran so high that there were occasions when the school children would break out during their classes in the singing of hymns. Little groups of spirit-filled children would meet in the schoolyard and hold testimony services. The whole city was feeling the power of the revival. It was not until high church authorities commenced to interfere that we felt led of the Lord to organize a separate and independent church. The glory of the Lord that had been with us in the old building accompanied the dear people as they crowded into the new one. Many years have passed since then but those precious people, to whom I used to minister, are still standing for the old truths, and worship God in Lodi Bethel Temple, dedicated to the preaching of the full Gospel.

Evangelism

About this time I felt the call of the Lord to go into evangelistic fields. It was a sad parting when I left Lodi. The church gave me a very beautiful testimonial and the Gospel Team gave me a huge analytical reference Bible with the following inscription on the flyleaf: "Presented to Charles S. Price by the members of the Lodi Gospel Team in appreciation of his loyalty and faithfulness to

Jesus Christ our Lord. Many are called but few are chosen. August 17, 1922." That Bible has travelled with me many, many miles and it is one of my most treasured possessions.

It seems incredible to believe that in one short year the Spirit of God would take me from a little California town and catapult me into great arenas where I would preach to vast throngs of ten thousand people night after night, but such was the case. What explanation is there for it, but that the Spirit of the Lord had fallen upon me! I was not new in the ministry. If it had been any ability that I possessed, why could I have not done this before? As a matter of fact, I never felt smaller in all my life. Ambition, pride, and self had been put upon the altar and the prayer of my heart was, "O Lord, have Thine own way with me." In my innermost being I was conscious of the Spirit of God leading me to say things and do things. There were times when I stood in amazement and awe before the result of my own ministry. All glory and honor be given to the Name of our adorable

Lord! What a precious and wonderful thing is this baptism with the Holy Ghost. I have proved its genuineness over and over again and tens of thousands of people have rejoiced with me in the falling of the old-time power.

So I want to take you by the hand and lead you down the corridors of the years, letting you look into some of the scenes of my ministry as an evangelist. My first meeting was at Ashland, Oregon. The Ministerial Union invited me and rented a building that seated more than the population of the town. It was soon packed to the doors. All the churches of the city were closed for the meetings and, having told the ministers that I was going to preach the whole truth, I proceeded to do so. The power fell. Hundreds were saved and hundreds were healed. The first person that I prayed with for bodily healing fell under the power of God. I, myself, was afraid. I prayed for the second one and the same thing happened. I trembled in the presence of the Lord; but both of them, rising to their feet and proclaiming they were healed, gave me courage and I went on praying. After that scores and scores would be prostrated under the power at one time. An adjacent building was rented so great became the crowds, and the meeting continued longer than its advertised time.

Albany, Oregon

From Ashland I went to Albany. One of my very closest friends, Rev. Thomas J. McCrossan, pastor of the United Presbyterian Church, had been down to the Ashland meeting and returned to Albany with reports of what the Lord had done. Dr. McCrossan became convinced that the whole movement was of God. He is the author of "The Bible —Its Christ, and Modernism" and many other marvelous books. The ministers engaged the Albany Armory and from the very first service it was packed to the doors. Quite often the crowd would stay in the building from ten o'clock in the morning until the time for the night meeting. We had to beg people, who were Christians, to stay away in order to allow the unsaved to find room. Practically the entire high school class gave their hearts to Jesus; and it has been reported that it was impossible to hold a public dance in town for one year after the campaign, because there were not unconverted girls enough with whom to dance. It was a mighty revival. I want to quote from Dr. McCrossan's own book at this point so that you might get some understanding of what happened in that meeting.

What Others Saw

"Dr. Price came to Albany with five churches behind him. At the very first service, Sunday afternoon, scores came to Christ. At each service, to the very close of the campaign, the altars were crowded with seekers. Many nights we had to vacate two, three and even four rows of chairs on the wide platform to accommodate the great overflow of seekers. Some of us ministers had been through campaigns with Moody, Torrey, Gipsy Smith, Wilbur Chapman, Biederwolf, F.B. Smith, French Oliver, Billy Sunday and other really great evangelists; but it was the unanimous opinion that we had never before found men and women under such tremendous conviction of sin as in this campaign. Very frequently from fifteen to twenty-five persons over sixty-five years of age were at the altar weeping their way to God. Here they found such a depth of conviction, the deepest by far they had ever experienced, that they knew for a surety this was the work of the Holy Spirit.

"At the first healing service in Albany I was fully convinced that God did heal the sick through prayer. The second person to be prayed for had a very large goiter. Dr. Price touched her forehead with oil, and then placing his hand upon her head offered a simple prayer that the Lord would then and there give her faith to accept. She is well today. We ministers felt withered hands and arms, time and again, which were cold and useless. Within an hour after being prayed for, those same hands and arms would be as warm as our own. Is it any wonder that we believe in divine healing?

"The last Saturday night was the greatest soul-winning service of the campaign. We ministers were all assisting Dr. Price, who was anointing some four hundred sick persons seated on the main floor, and we followed to pray for those anointed. While thus engaged, God's Spirit took possession of the meeting. Without any invitation being given, sinners began to flock to the altar; old people seventy years of age and scores of young people. Young converts came forward bringing their weeping companions. Soon the altar and the whole stage were crowded with seekers, and everywhere in the house people began to fall under the strange power of God. We preachers had read of such scenes in Finney's meetings, but we had never expected such experiences ourselves. We then knew what Christ meant when He said, John 14:12, '...

greater works than these shall ye do, because I go unto my Father.' This revealed the long forgotten truth, viz.: that Christ predicted there would be an augmenting rather than a diminishing of supernatural power after He left the earth. Such predicted power one sees in Dr. Price's meetings. As a result of our meetings hundreds were saved. One church received over one hundred members, another seventy-five, another sixty and another fifty, but most of the converts were outside of this city.

British Columbia

"At Roseburg, Eugene, Victoria and Vancouver, B. C., this same wonderful soul-winning power was evident. At one afternoon service in Roseburg, Rev. Dr. Sipprell, of Victoria, and I, saw thirty-five persons from sixty-five to eighty years of age kneeling at the altar seeking Christ. The oldest ministers in all these cities have admitted to me that in all their experience they have never seen God's soul-winning power so displayed. In both the Victoria and Vancouver campaigns there were days when from seven hundred to one thousand persons came to the altar, all under the same tremendous conviction of sin."

I have quoted from the pen of Dr. McCrossan because I know my readers will appreciate the opinion of one so well known in the religious world. How wonderful was my Lord to take a self-willed, proud preacher like I had been and fill him with His Spirit! We give Him the glory for it all.

From Albany we went to the First Methodist Church of Eugene. Once again the power fell. We were forced to move to the spacious armory and that too became crowded to the doors. Out of that meeting there was built Lighthouse Temple with one of the most spacious auditoriums in the entire full gospel movement. During the Eugene campaign miracles of healing occurred that shook the entire countryside, and denominational preachers were filled with the Holy Ghost.

Next we moved to Roseburg and it was there, while preaching in the armory, that the Lord opened the doors of Canada to my ministry.

Many Healed

Dr. W.J. Sipprell, pastor of the Metropolitan Methodist Church of Victoria, had heard about the meetings through a letter written by Mr. Donald McCrossan, son of the minister whom I have quoted. He came down to investigate and, going back to Victoria, brought the matter before his church and invited me to conduct a campaign there. After very earnest prayer I accepted the invitation. The Metropolitan Methodist Church of Victoria has a seating capacity of approximately three thousand people. Before we had been there many days a series of miraculous healings occurred that shook the town. Outstanding among them were the healings of the Rev. W.J. Knott, a Methodist minister who was healed of a tremendous goiter that disappeared, before the eyes of the congregation. Then came the healing of Miss Ruby Dimick. She was the daughter of a Methodist minister and her healing from paralysis and a crippled condition was so evident that it awakened the province. Newspapers all over Canada and the United States printed the story. The Literary Digest printed an account of the case. True it was that opinions differed as to how it was done, but still the fact remained the healing had taken place and a crippled girl had been made whole. Tens of thousands of people in British Columbia knew that it was the power of God.

Then came the great campaign in Vancouver, British Columbia. Scores of churches closed for the meeting. A great chorus was organized and a body of 300 ushers trained to handle the crowds. Mr. Frank Patrick, the owner of the arena, says, "I kept track of the crowds. In three weeks 250,000 people went into that arena to hear Mr. Price preach." Some idea of the congregations might be gleaned from the

Daily World: "Ten thousand people crowded into the arena, and a crowd of between 4,000 and 5,000 outside, unable to gain admittance...Outside automobiles were packed for over a mile in every direction, while ambulances were lined up in front of the arena, and street cars extended for blocks. In and out among the vehicles the crowds surged from shortly after 6 o'clock, the doors having been closed at that hour, when the arena was seen to be packed. Inside, tier upon tier, to the highest row, right under the roof, the crowd was packed. Firemen vainly strove to keep the aisles clear, but even the stairway to the choir seats was crowded. Many people brought camp chairs and found sitting room wherever they could; others stood for hours, anxious to see the evangelist at work. People in all walks of life, business men, professional men, laborers and tradesmen were packed elbow to elbow in the boxes and balconies."

Not of Man

It is with a feeling of deep humiliation and eternal gratitude to God that I recount these events. There is a sense in which I dislike putting them down in this record, for fear that some should think that the ego is asserting itself too much. God forbid. I am only a sinner saved by grace; and it is for the glory of the Lord alone that I tell of the marvelous things that the Lord has done. I am reciting these events in order to show you what God can do with a man who will lay himself on the altar and seek until he is filled with the Holy Ghost. If there was any power in the meetings, it was the power of God. It was not mine. As a matter of fact, I rejoiced on the days when God took the meetings out of my hands and manifested Himself in such marvelous and glorious ways that all the people wondered! I do not feel that this volume would be complete were I to omit that remarkable meeting, probably the most wonderful of my life, that was held among the

Chinese of the City of Victoria. As I write I am transported in spirit back to those days. Let me take you by the hand and together we will walk down the corridors of the years to that eventful night.

9
FIGHTING THE GOOD FIGHT

The meeting in the great Arena is over. The crowds are surging out of the building and singing as they go the strains of the hymns they love. It has been hot in the building, and all who have worked so hard are weary and tired from the efforts of the day; for already three services have been held and scores of people prayed for. It is the time when people can rest; a time when our weary bodies call for sleep. A car is waiting at the door of the Arena, and as we jump into it we are welcomed by the Police Commissioner who tells us that Chinatown is agog with anticipation and eager with the expectancy of hope.

Down through the city we go until at last the car draws up in front of the door of an old Chinese theater. With a burly policeman leading the way, we brave the stifling atmosphere and at last are greeted by the sight of hundreds of Orientals packed in every nook and cranny of the building. A number of Chinese mission workers and an interpreter are already on the platform and inform us that some of the people have been there for three and four hours waiting for the opening hymn. The service commences with the singing of hymns, most of the people singing in Chinese and some singing in English: but the message that rises from the walls of the old Chinese theater to the Throne of Grace is one language when it reaches the heart of God. The preliminary service is over, a simple story is told; sentence by sentence, for the interpreter must think of his words. It is the story of a Cross, an emblem of suffering and shame. The story of a Christ who died on that Cross, not only for the soul of the Caucasian, but to enter the heart of

China.

After the message is over, the altar call is given, and a sight perhaps unparalleled in Chinese work on the Pacific Coast is witnessed at that call. "Every man and woman in this building who will here and now accept Christ as their Savior and renounce their heathen religion and come to this altar to pray, put up your hands and ask for the prayers of the people who love our Lord."

Nearly every hand in the building is raised. Dr. Osterhout, who has charge of the Chinese work for the Methodist Church of Canada, has come to the front of the platform with an exclamation of amazement. A moment or two later the Chinese are swarming onto the platform. They fill it once with men, then again with women, and then again with men, and once again with women, until four separate altar calls have been given in the one meeting and the building is ringing with praises unto the Lord.

Winning Chinese

I would like at this point to give you the impression of my dear friend, Dr. Thomas J. McCrossan, who was present at that meeting and who told me later that it was the greatest service he ever attended in his life. Under the heading "Winning Heathen Chinese to Christ," Dr. McCrossan says: "While in Victoria I witnesses a sight that convinced me, as nothing else had done, that Dr. Price was a mighty man of God. In a theater I heard him address 900 heathen Chinamen through an interpreter. He told the story of the creation, fall and redemption of man, how that the Lord Jesus came to earth and died that God might be just and the justifier of him who believed in Jesus. When through, he offered a short prayer, and then gave an invitation through the interpreter for sinners to come to Christ. More than four hundred made a start and the altar, comprising three rows of chairs all the width of the theater, was filled three different times. Three returned Chinese missionaries, the three resident missionaries, and Rev. Osterhout (superintendent of Methodist Chinese work) spoke with these seekers. They told us they had never seen men and women under such deep conviction of sin, and they felt sure most all of them understood clearly what they had done."

Two Gifts

At the conclusion of the services in Victoria two gifts were given to me as a token of the love of the people. I am human enough to prize such things very highly, although I am somewhat bewildered as to which one I prize the more. One was a beautiful medal of gold with the following inscription: "Presented to Charles S. Price, Evangelist, by the Chinese Christians of Victoria in deep appreciation of his labors and services among our people." That medal or gold is often looked at and prayers ascend from my heart to God for Him to keep those dear Chinese always and ever under the blood.

The other gift of which I speak was a resolution passed by the ministerial association and reads as follows: "In respect to the evangelistic campaign conducted in this city from April 8th to April 29th, by Rev. Dr. C. S. Price, a minister of the Congregational Church of California:

"We, the members of the Ministerial Association of the City of Victoria, desire to make the following statement:

"Having had ample opportunity throughout the course of the campaign to observe the methods and to hear the addresses in connection with the said campaign, we would commend, without reserve, the fine Christian spirit, the transparent character, and evident devotion of the evangelist in all his work. We would also remark upon his deeply sympathetic attitude towards the various churches, as well as towards all persons who might in any way differ from him in doctrinal belief.

"We regard his evangelistic message as

strong, persuasive, and scriptural; wholly devoid of levity of superficiality, and always marked by a passionate desire to exalt the Lord Jesus Christ, as the Son of God, and the Savior of men, in a manner which carried conviction and blessing to the hearts of his hearers.

"We would place on record our gratitude to God for the splendid spiritual results obtained, and our appreciation of the methods adopted by the evangelist to bring people to the point of decision, both as to the acceptance of Jesus Christ for salvation, and the seeking of the baptism of the Holy Spirit as bringing to them greater power for service.

"We would also state that the prayers offered for the healing of the sick have been answered in many cases that can be verified, and that there are many instances where bodily disease and infirmity have apparently disappeared, and the persons concerned claim to be perfectly well.

"We, therefore, heartily commend the work of Rev. C.S. Price as an evangelist, to all our churches, and pray that God's continued blessing may rest upon him and his co-workers in all their efforts to promote the interests of the Kingdom of God.

"(Signed) William Stevenson,
on behalf of the association."

One year after the close of the Victoria meeting, I returned again to the city and held another great campaign in the same arena with the same churches cooperating. Then came the great meeting in Vancouver with its tremendous interest, enormous crowds, and the falling of the old-time power. The closing night of that campaign is one that will live long in my memory. Over one thousand people were prayed for for bodily healing and I was so tired at the conclusion of the service that I could hardly keep on my feet. It is undoubtedly true that thousands of lives were won to the Lord Jesus Christ. It certainly pays to be filled with the Holy Ghost!

10

THE PASSING YEARS

It is impossible to record in detail the events of all the years that have passed, but I do want to mention a few of the outstanding campaigns and give God the glory for the victories that were won. From Vancouver, I went with my party to Calgary, a very beautiful town in Alberta, and rented the great horse show building for the revival meeting. Not many of the local churches closed to help in the meetings, but that did not seem to hinder the sweep of victory that God gave us. It was during this meeting that I felt led by the Spirit one night to answer my own altar call. My heart was hungry for more of God. When the devil tried to tell me that the people would misunderstand my action, I rebuked him. With tears streaming down my face, I asked the people to pray that God would melt me and break me so that He might be everything and that I might be nothing. So sweetly the Lord visited me that night with an outpouring of His glorious presence that I shall never forget through time and eternity.

I have been to Calgary four different times and have thousands of dear and loyal friends there. It was in Calgary that I first met my dear co-worker, Charles Jackson, who travelled with me so long and proved of such value in conducting the campaigns.

Great as have been the victories in British Columbia, we found even greater congregations and a mightier sweep of glory in Edmonton. The great ice arena, seating 12,000 people, was so crowded that on one occasion people climbed onto the roof and tried to break their way in. They even smashed windows and then threw money into the arena to pay for the damage they had done. It was in this Edmonton meeting that so many lives were dedicated to God, and a large number of people are ministers on the home and foreign fields as a result of the campaign. When I tried the following year to rent the Edmonton arena once again, I was informed by the City Council that I could not use the building unless I took out an accident insurance policy covering everybody that entered the arena. One of the officials with whom I dealt, said, "We do not want a repetition of those enormous crowds that assembled last year for the services."

Then came the great campaigns of Brandon and Winnipeg. We were forced to move out of the Winnipeg Arena into the Amphitheater to accommodate the congregations. The very opening night of this service, according to the Winnipeg Free Press, "Over eight thousand people crowded the Amphitheater to capacity last night to hear the evangelist, Dr. Charles S. Price." What the paper did not know was that I had to climb in through the kitchen window to get into the building, for the crowd was so great at the door that I could not make my way through the throng. It was a common sight to see one hundred to four hundred kneeling at the altar in a single meeting in some of those large arena campaigns. Even though many years have passed, I am still corresponding with people who made their start for the Lord Jesus Christ in those glorious, wonderful days.

My life became just one evangelistic meeting after another. A flaming, consuming passion burned within my heart. I wanted to win souls for Jesus. I wanted to preach the Gospel so that everybody throughout the countryside could hear it. I refused to take pledges in my meetings for myself or for expenses for fear that someone would think that the campaigns were nothing but a commercial enterprise. By day and by night my prayer to God was, "Oh Lord, give me souls—give me souls." So it was I preached until there were times when I would collapse at the close of the services from sheer fatigue. Church systems began to organize against the movement and circulate many peculiar reports about me and my ministry. If these men could only have read my heart they never would have put a straw in the way to impede my work for God; but to reply has never been my policy. I just kept on preaching the Gospel, and telling the sweetest story ever told. In my heart I knew there was not a soul in the audience that Jesus could not save. I knew there was not a sick body that He could not heal. I knew that there was not a question but what my Lord could answer. I knew that there was not a problem that He could not solve. That fired me up. It gave me zeal and strength to go on when the battle was hard.

When the Power Fell

Time marched on and there came the great meetings in Toronto, Minneapolis, Duluth, East St. Louis and Belleville. Perhaps I should put on this record, for the glory of the Lord, a few facts regarding the Belleville, Illinois, meeting. While not as large as the Vancouver meeting; while not as well attended, perhaps, as the great campaigns in Edmonton and other cities have been; yet, in some respects, it was the most marvelous meeting of my ministry up to that date. At the end of the campaign in East St. Louis, the Rev. Mr. Humphrey, pastor of the Jackson Methodist Episcopal Church of Belleville, invited me to preach in his church during a Sunday morning service. It was that meeting that opened the doors of Belleville to my ministry. The Moose auditorium was rented for the services and the very first meeting saw the place crowded and hundreds turned away.

As the days went on the crowds increased, until at last it became necessary to hold THREE MEETINGS A DAY. The afternoon crowd would fill the building and then the doors would be locked. The night crowd would gather at an early hour, and at 5:30 the doors would be again opened. The service would begin at six o'clock, and after that service was over, the crowd would be made to leave by the police and fire departments and the next crowd would fill the building for the

8:30 service. Even then people would be left outside. We kept this up until our physical strength broke under the strain, and we had to return to the regular schedule of two meetings a day.

The crowds still came. As my auto would drive up to the reserved parking space, a roar would go up outside, "Please let us in, Dr. Price...please, can we come in tonight?" Then another, "We have driven a hundred miles and got here just too late...can we get in?" I would have said "Yes," but, there on the steps was the strong arm of the law. The local fire department handled the situation for a while, then the STATE FIRE CHIEF came down to handle the crowds, and see that no one was hurt and that the fire rules of the state were enforced. Praise the Lord for that meeting. It was glorious, entrancing and inspiring and we give to our dear Lord all the glory.

But the best is yet to come. Will you rejoice with us in this fact: that during the last TEN DAYS of the great Belleville campaign there was an average of over ONE THOUSAND

CONVERSIONS EVERY DAY! ONE THOUSAND A DAY!

Hallelujah! That is a conservative estimate. The preachers would weep...the workers were unable to handle the souls at the altar...the whole altar was so jammed that the workers could not move around...the aisles would fill clear to the back of the building...kneeling figures...tears...prayers...songs...and shouts. NEVER HAVE I SEEN ANYTHING LIKE IT IN ALL MY EXPERIENCE. It was wonderful. Glory to Jesus!

At last I had to turn the whole building into an altar, and one old Free Methodist preacher, Rev. Bresee, who had lived and preached there for fifty years, said that never in all Belleville's history had so many souls come to Christ. The fire department and its men caught the spirit. Night after night the red car of the fire chief would be there in front of the building and one of our most enthusiastic workers was the fire chief himself. The motorcycle police were on hand, helping to park the automobiles; and they, too, entered into the spirit of the great campaign.

How we give God the glory for such things as this! How different my life was in such a ministry, than it had been before I was filled with the Holy Spirit! If there is any one thing that I shall praise the Lord for when I see my blessed Savior one of these wonderful days, it is the fact that I received the light of full Gospel truth in time enough to give some years of my life in service to Jesus. What a day it will be for me when I lay my trophies at His feet! How did it all begin, you ask? Back in that Sunday school room in the Baptist Church in San Jose when a recently born-again preacher cried out for the old-time power and God answered by fire.

By this time the Lord had led me very definitely to start my magazine, "Golden Grain," which is one of the dearest treasures of my heart. Through winter and summer, good times and hard times, depression and no depression, "Golden Grain" has gone on its world mission of carrying the full Gospel message to the uttermost parts of the earth. I commenced to write the magazine in prayer, dedicating each number as it came off the press, to the salvation of souls and the healing of bodies. I still do. I believe that is why God has blessed it. It has been one of the most important factors in my ministry and undoubtedly has led thousands of souls to Jesus Christ.

Ministers of various denominations have been writing me through the years regarding divine healing and the baptism of the Holy Ghost and in the files of my office I have many letters telling of how God has answered prayer in the lives of these preachers. The publishing of a magazine by an evangelist who was spending ten months out of every twelve on the road was an added task, but God gave me strength.

One would think that the steady grind of campaign would proved monotonous, but it did not in my case. I have guarded very carefully against becoming a professional evangelist. I did not want to carry around a few sermons in my briefcase and deliver the same messages over and over again. There were illustrations the Lord had blessed that I could repeat and there were sermons that I could give the second time, but I determine by the grace of God that I would keep burning on the altar of my heart the desire to see men saved. More than once I have looked through some little peep hole at the congregation and then just before I went into the pulpit I would fall trembling on my face before God. "Dear Jesus," I would pray, "out there are hundreds, perhaps thousands of men and women who are lost. Oh, my Lord, help me to give them the message that they need—help me to preach with power—help me to make You so beautiful and so wonderful that everybody here will fall in love with You and find salvation." Little did the audience realize it, but more than once I would have to cry out to God to give me strength and courage to face the multitude. Then I have seen them break before I have had a chance to give an altar call. I have watched them come down the aisles to kneel at the foot of the Cross, so great was the conviction upon their hearts.

Tabernacle Days

But the days sped by. The cost of buildings became a serious problem for me to face and solve. One day the Lord very definitely directed me to build my first huge wooden tabernacle. In recent years I have been using these tremendous frame buildings in cities throughout the countryside, particularly in the Pacific Northwest. Yakima and Bellingham both have had wooden tabernacles. Two have been erected on different occasions in the city of Seattle; while Tacoma has built three for my evangelistic ministry.

I believe a very unusual and unique record was established just a year or two ago in the city of Tacoma. Inside of two calendar years I had built three tabernacles and held three campaigns. During those two years we were in meetings in the one town for six months. That means that one day out of every four I was preaching twice a day in a specially constructed tabernacle over the two-year period. We give God the glory for the fact that the closing meetings found the tabernacle filled and that congregations of one thousand would meet on weekday mornings to hear Bible expositions as I tried to unfold the Word of God.

It was here that my collection of treasure increased. I was so deeply moved and touched by the incident that brought this treasure to me that I feel I ought to record it here. I had noticed in the audience a Jewish man and woman sitting together on more than one occasion. They were typical Jewish people. He was a man with a beard and she was a woman with a shawl wrapped around her head. More than once I had observed them kneeling at the altar.

One night they came to me after the service with a very reverent expression on their faces. Suddenly the Jewish brother took my hand and then kissed it. I knew they were Russians, and I also knew that such was the custom of their country. Then that dear Jewish woman got out of her purse a little golden box. It was beautifully made, and in it was the Jewish name of God. She told me that it was the custom in Russia for the orthodox Jewish people to nail this little box of gold upon the door post of their home. Even the nails were solid gold. It signified that the people who lived in the house were followers of the God of Abraham, and of Isaac, and of Jacob. It also served as a constant reminder for them to worship God.

I tried to refuse her gift, but she insisted on my keeping it. Tears coursed down her cheeks as she said, "I do not need the name of God in a box of gold—for He has written His name on my heart." And then smiling looking into my face she said, "My brother, how I love Jesus!" So I came away with my little box of gold, but what was more precious—infinitely more precious—the testimony of that dear man and woman—ringing in my ears. Five of their children are now on the firing line for the Lord Jesus Christ.

The Lord has also led me during recent years into some of the great camp-meetings of the nation as camp evangelist. Four years in succession I was called to the beautiful Lake Geneva Bible Conference and Camp Meeting. The ground is situated on a lovely lake in the heart of Minnesota. For two years I was the speaker at the Eastern District Camp-Meeting with its great throng that came from all over the East to the campgrounds at Green Lane, Pennsylvania. Through the courtesy of my ministerial brethren, I have conducted camp-meetings also in Iowa, Illinois, Washington, Nebraska and other states. It has been hard work, but the Lord Himself has given me the strength.

11
MEETINGS ABROAD

One night in 1933 I was kneeling in prayer before the Lord. I had just completed the sermons and articles for my monthly magazine, "Golden Grain," and was asking the blessing of the Lord upon them as I sent them forth. I was very tired in body, and was praying about His will regarding a vacation time for rest. I was still on my knees when a letter was put in my hands. It was from one of my brethren in England, who was asking me to go back to the end that gave me birth as a speaker at the National Conference to be held in the city of London. He also included invitations from Norway, Sweden and Finland. I re-read the letter on my knees, and then left the whole matter before the Lord.

Door after door seemed to open, and the dear Lord made it very clear that it was His will that we should make the trip. Nothing in the world could have blessed me more. It had long been an ambition of mine to go back to the place where I had spent my boyhood days and give my testimony for Jesus. A few days passed by and another letter arrived—this time from Egypt. I saw in it the hand of God.

My dear friends, Mr. and Mrs. J.L. Barneson, who had been such a help to me in the publishing of "Golden Grain," consented to go with me and my party, and it was in February, 1934, that we sailed for Europe. I took my own car with me, for when a number of people travel together in foreign lands, gasoline is cheaper than railroad fare. Besides that, it helps you to see the countryside. You get away from the beaten tracks that tourists ordinarily follow. We landed at Cherbourgh in France and motored to Marseilles. Then we took a steamer across the Mediterranean to Alexandria, Egypt. We motored down the historic Nile to marvelous old Cairo. How I enjoyed the services I conducted there! I can still see the smiling, dark-skinned faces looking up at me; as, through an interpreter, I told them of the glory of my risen Lord. Scores and scores of them testified to being filled with the Holy Ghost. Peter was right when he declared, "The promise is unto you and to your children and to them that are afar off."

I motored from Cairo to Jerusalem, crossing the wilderness of Sinai. It was one of the great adventure-journeys of my life. Then came my ministry in Jerusalem and visits to the places made sacred by my Lord. How I treasured those golden days! How memory takes me back now to the sunlight playing on Jordan and to the peaceful quiet that came over my should as I drank of the waters from Jacob's well! How well do I remember the symphonies that were played by the waves of Galilee as they beat upon the rocky shore at old Capernaum. The tears come even now when I think of the moment when I stooped down and went into the sepulcher where they put the body of my Lord. Shall I ever forget Calvary—and will the vision of the winding, narrow streets of old Jerusalem ever be erased from my memory and mind? I was fascinated with Palestine.

Stockholm

The meetings in Norway and Sweden I shall never forget. What a church that is in Stockholm! Five thousand members, and every one of them real, living members. Brother Peters, the pastor, does not believe in carrying a lot of useless, dead timber around just to make up a large church membership. I wish I had the ability to describe to you just what that great Stockholm church is like. Notwithstanding the tremendous seating capacity (close to 4,000) everyone in the building is comparatively near you; and your voice can be heard even though you should speak in a whisper.

The platform on which the pulpit stands is

the largest we have ever seen. What altar calls I had at the conclusion of my sermons! The prayer rooms below the main auditorium would be so crowded that other rooms had to be opened as the people came to pray. Imagine the 500 room so crowded we could not get any more in it, as the people waited before the Lord. Then the 120 room would be filled, and the praying crowd would overflow from that. It was indeed such a pleasure and privilege to minister to people who would respond like that.

There is a real revival in Sweden. Many of the Baptist preachers have been filled with the Holy Ghost. Some of the Baptist colleges are teaching the glorious truth of the infilling of the Spirit. There are some villages in Sweden where every man, woman and child in the village has had a full Gospel experience. Just imagine that! It is hard to believe, and yet it is absolutely true.

Then my mind goes to the day when my steamer sailed majestically up the smooth waters of the Oslo Fjord. The tall mountains rise to the right and to the left, reflecting and glowing in the water at our feet. What scenery! What a glorious array of changing views! Beautiful waterways seemed to present themselves with every successive mile, and long before we reached Oslo every member of the party was saying, "Is not Norway beautiful!" We were admirably entertained by our dear friend, Rev. T.B. Barratt, who is the pastor of the church of "Philadelphia," the home of Pentecost in Norway. Brother Barratt's name is known to everybody in the city. Formerly a Methodist preacher of prominence in Norway, he received the baptism with the Holy Spirit, and God has used him in lighting Pentecostal fires in various countries throughout Northern Europe.

The opening service found the spacious building crowded to the doors. People were standing in the eager congregation. Then they commenced to sing! Never shall we forget that music. There is something plaintive—a predominance of minor strains—in so many of the Norwegian hymns. They reach down to the very depths of your heart. A splendid stringed orchestra would every once in a while carry through the verse and chorus without the aid of the human voices; then, suddenly, the whole congregation would catch up the melody, and the building would ring with the praises of God. How I thank God for my visit to wonderful Scandinavia!

Back to dear old England! Years before, a mother—just before her death—had dedicated her boy to the service of the Lord. That boy was back—back after years and years of sojourn in a foreign land. It was Sunday night, and an occasion I shall never, never forget. It was the old church, the church where my mother and father had worshipped in the years gone by. In that church my uncles and aunts and grandparents had preached and sung the glory of the Lord. On the hillside, less than a mile away, most of them were awaiting the glorious day when the dead in Christ shall arise. Their message had been given—their testimony had been spoken—

their race had been run. Inside that church were scores and scores of the younger generation of the members of my family.

In my heart I knew of what they were thinking, as they waited for me to mount the pulpit steps. In my heart I knew what my dear father and mother were thinking as they waited anxiously for their son to make his appearance. Others of the remaining relatives of my family were waiting too; and I believed I knew what was in their hearts. I know what was in mine. "Dear Jesus," I said, "I thank You for this day. For years I have lived for it —for years I have prayed for it—and now it has come to pass. Help me to preach—help me to be true to the message."

One of the stewards opened a little door, and I tremblingly mounted the pulpit steps. I looked out over the congregation, nearly all of whom I knew. Boys with whom I had played in the years gone by were men now with their families by their side. I looked for old familiar faces—but some of them were gone, never to be seen again until our Lord unites us in the realms of eternal day. I glanced down and saw the face of my father. He looked up at me and smiled through the tear drops. I stepped to the pulpit, "All Hail the Power of Jesus' Name." I am wondering if somebody else was not leaning over the battlements of heaven, listening to me preach in the old home church that Sunday night.

A few days sped by and I was in London. The Lord had made it possible for me to preach in an Episcopal College, overlooking the historic Thames. The place was crowded to the doors, and people were unable to find even standing room. I led my old father down the aisle and we were both seated together on the platform. Just before I rose to preach, the Holy Spirit whispered in my heart the message for that night, "The Potter and the Clay."

When the service was over, I received another gift. It was not a little golden box, such as I received from the Jewish woman; neither was it a medal of gold, such as the Chinese gave me in far away Victoria. It was nothing that I could handle, nothing that I could see; but it was one of the greatest gifts I have ever received in all my life. It was a word from my father. One of the English preachers had leaned over to him and said, "We are happy to have him with us tonight as our preacher, Mr. Price." My father looked into his eyes and said, "And I am proud to have him as my son." I looked into his face, and there passed before me the events of the years gone by—his prayers, his love, his sacrifices—that was why those words meant so much to me then, and why they mean so much to me now; but I am waiting for another word. That will be the crowning word of them all. It is when Jesus will say to me, "Well done."

ADDENDUM TO SECOND EDITION

So it is, as the second edition of "The Story of My Life" goes to press, I am still on the firing line for Jesus. Many campaigns have been held in America and lands across the sea since the last edition was printed. As a matter of fact, I have preached the Gospel of the Lord Jesus Christ once again on four continents. I can still testify that the greatest joy of my life is to see souls saved. The campaigns in the various parts of the country met with wonderful response. We particularly enjoyed the meeting in Duquesne, Pennsylvania.

At the close of the last service, Rev. Harry Lee Crawford arose and presented the following testimonial to Evangelist Charles S. Price:

Duquesne, Pennsylvania, January 24, 1937

"Whereas...this city has been blessed during the past three weeks by the presence of Dr. Charles S. Price and party, of Pasadena, Calif., who through the services of Divine worship and praise that they have led, have brought inestimable riches to this community;

"And whereas, Dr. Price has exemplified in our midst the three-fold ministry of the Master in ministering to spirit, mind and body by preaching, teaching and healing;

"And whereas, we have learned to love him as one, who with the spirit of the Master, in a dignified and yet powerful manner, has proclaimed the glad tidings of the Gospel:

"Therefore, be it resolved, that as pastors of the churches of Duquesne, we hereby record our gratitude and appreciation of the self-sacrificing labors of Dr. Price and his party; and be it further resolved, that we commend the sane and sound evangelistic campaigns of Dr. Price to all true followers of the Lord everywhere, and pray God's richest blessings upon him and all his fellow-workers."

The above was signed by the Rev. R.A. Graybill, of the First Christian Church; the Rev. George F. Hambleton, of the First Baptist Church; the Rev. Harry L. Crawford, of the First Presbyterian Church; the Rev. Alfred J. Herman, of the Grace Reformed Church; the Rev. Andrew P. Slabey, of the Congregational Church; the Rev. S.E. Brown, of the First Methodist Episcopal Church; the Rev. F.A. Alford, of the Zion Lutheran Church, and the Rev. C.W. Walker Jr., of the First English Lutheran Church.

ADDENDUM TO THIRD EDITION

And now this third edition of "The Story of My Life" goes to press. How good God is! Since the last edition of this volume was written, my heavenly Father has opened the doors to my ministry once again on the far flung continents of the world. Memories flood my mind of the late visit to Norway and to Sweden with the great meetings here. I am thinking of the ministry I was privileged to give to my brethren in Egypt and once again sailing to Palestine where my Savior walked and talked years ago; the Easter Sunday I spent in Smyrna and the trip through the Dardanelles into historic Turkey. I can still see Patmos and Rhodes and Tripoli. What a privilege to witness for Jesus in lands afar! There is Damascus and Beirut and later the journey through Italy across the heart of Europe.

But in closing this volume I think my greatest gratitude to God would be for the privilege He has accorded me of writing my magazine, "Golden Grain." It now goes around the world. For eighteen years, I have been writing the sermons which have sent my written ministry into a multitude of homes, and the printed page has been the means of leading thousands to Christ and Savior and Healer. I am writing today in the full knowledge that my ministry of the printed page now exceeds in influence and power the ministry of the preached word from pulpit and platform. How good and kind is our loving Lord! How much I appreciate the friendship and prayers of that multitude of people who have participated in my ministry for the cause of Christ and the everlasting gospel.

How many years of service I have left,

should Jesus tarry, I do not know; but I am rejoicing in the long list of my sons and daughters in the Lord, who are preaching His blessed truth all over the home land, on the continents afar, and on the islands of the sea. But for my hope of heaven, I am not trusting in what little I may have done; but I am counting on the blood He shed when He died for me on Calvary to redeem my soul. After all, it is not what we do for Jesus, but what He has done for us which makes our salvation sure.

Thus concludes your book.

Be sure to visit us online for more of the best Christian books ever written.

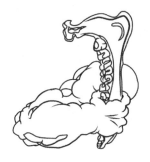

We've got several other books by
Dr. Charles S. Price,
and plenty more from
others like him.

http://JawboneDigital.com/Price